Copyright © Nicholas Maze, 20
may be reproduced or transmitt
mechanical, including photocopying, recording, or by any information storage
and retrieval system, without permission in writing from the publisher.

King Writing

PO Box 767

Flint, MI 48501

TRUTH: Discovering Who You Are and the Power You Possess

Designed by snirz94, fiverr.com

Publisher's Note: This is a work of fiction. Names, characters, places, and incidents either are the product of the author's imagination, or are used fictitiously, and any resemblance to actual persons, living or dead, events, or locales is entirely coincidental.

ISBN: 978-1-71658-882-2

Maze, Nicholas L., TRUTH: Discovering Who You Are and the Power You Possess

Special Sales

These books are available at special discounts for bulk purchases. Special editions, including personalized covers, excerpts of existing books, and corporate imprints, can be created in large quantities for special needs. For more information e-mail

nicholas@whitecollarwoman.com

TRUTH

Discovering Who You Are and the Power You Possess

Nicholas L. Maze

I dedicate this book to all the inspiration and support that motivates me to continue writing.

Table of Content

Chapter One: Truth 1

Chapter Two: Knowledge 5

Chapter Three: Who You Are 10

Chapter Four: Communication 16

Chapter Five: Meditation 22

Chapter Six: Inner Communication 26

Chapter Seven: Vision 31

Chapter Eight: A Leader 37

Chapter Nine: Roadblocks 41

Chapter Ten: Negativity 46

Chapter Eleven: Limitations 52

Chapter Twelve: Your Source 56

Chapter Thirteen: Beliefs 63

Chapter Fourteen: Why Do We Fail 69

Chapter Fifteen: Brain Power 74

Chapter Sixteen: Affirming 79

Chapter Seventeen: Instant Change 83

Chapter Eighteen: Who You Are 91

Chapter One

Truth

Never. Never have I been more led to write a book like this in my entire life. The only book that came close was my financial book *EXIT: How to Leave Debt Forever*. It made sense. I was at a stage in my life where I was focused on money. This included starting my own business and investing. *EXIT* was the second book I had written. My first book, *White Collar Woman* was a fiction story that focused on a woman in the corporate world. Although it was a test to see if I was able to publish a book, I genuinely enjoyed writing *White Collar Woman*. I always had a desire to write, but never knew my purpose. I enjoyed *White Collar Woman* so much I eventually wrote four additional books and created my own series. I also wrote a book on religion. Now that I look back, it is interesting to see where I am today.

My writings began to show my maturity. While writing my fiction stories, I kept going into areas I was concerned about and I felt deserved a platform. Witnessing how so many people mistreated money and misunderstood it led me to write *EXIT*. I am not sure how many people comprehended what direction I was going in, but I received positive reviews. After *EXIT*, I placed my attention on three fiction books. Then I went into my book on religion, *Deleting GOD: Failures in the Church Community*. There were some things in my religious world that I felt strongly about and I wanted it to have its own platform, so once again, I followed my passion. I am not sure how it was received, but I was proud of what I created.

There are two things I learned about the nonfiction books I wrote:

1. I had passion.

2. I did not fear what others had to say.

It was something that I eventually lost in my writing career. Part of it had to do with changes in my health, while the majority of it dealt with no longer believing in myself. With starting this book, I was preparing to write and release the sixth installment in the *White Collar Woman* series. One of the things I discovered while writing was this book could play an important role in the way we live. This led to the title, *Truth*. There was something inside of me pushing to get out.

On the other side of the coin, I kept watching my life change. I kept seeing the maturity in me growing. I experienced things I had never experienced, back when I was writing my first book. It was beyond physical change. It was a mental and spiritual change. Although I have had some great experiences in life, nothing could compare to the experiences I was now having. It was a similar drive that led me to *EXIT*. It was a similar passion that led me to *Deleting GOD*. Only now, it was multiplied. Now, I was at a crossing road. I could no longer walk the yellow line and try to get by without being hit. Now I had to choose the truth. I believed what I had experienced and was taught in the past, or now I believed what I was currently experiencing and being taught.

It is amazing to see the differences in my writings. Working on my latest fiction, I would have to pause and generate ideas on what to write. Working on Truth, the content just seemed to flow out. This is confirmation of where I should be. Whoever you are, thank you for even taking the time to read this work. I know this is a unique subject, so there may be some questions. Even as I write this, I still have questions myself. But I am proud to say it becomes clearer and clearer every day. This is simply my perspective on this journey we call life. It may not be exactly what you want it to be, but that is a great thing. It should not be. We are all different. My writing is designed to reach those that may need some help in understanding what their purpose and goals are in life, while also generating a gray area for discussion.

Chapter Two

Knowledge

There is an open end of questions with life. All of us so badly want to know the meaning, the truth. Since the beginning of time, it has been the goal.

"Why am I here?"

"Why did this happen?"

"How do I change?"

The list goes on and on. In all honesty, none of us have the answer. There has not been one person that knew it all, but they still shared what knowledge they had. Therefore, we can never judge someone because their knowledge is limited to what they have experienced and what they have been taught. We cannot pretend as if one person knows it all. Even some of the greatest writings we swear by are limited to a person's understanding. It is not the beginning and end of anything. Life is constantly changing. There is no way to tell you what the end of life will be. And the beginning is limited to life here on earth. A person cannot even say what happened before the age of 3, let alone tell you what happened in the beginning of time.

Everything is viewed through that person's perspective. We limit who we are when we limit ourselves to others. Someone tells you how A got to Z. If you believe in your heart this is so, then you will swear by it and it becomes you. This is tied to every belief in life. It never existed in your life, until you believed it. I clearly noticed how what I believed appeared in my life. My life became my belief. It goes deeper and displays the power we possess. Therefore, you can go years without being or living a certain way. Then one day, you experience or witness something that changes your entire view on life. And whatever is tied to that experience channels your heart and changes your mind. The issue is that we place our attention on the thing or person and believe this to be the reason for what has occurred in our lives. This takes us back to our beliefs. It is amazing that you can believe in something so strongly that it eventually becomes you. This is tied to every aspect of our lives. It was not you. It became you.

This is what we must focus on. It was not you, but it became you. This would have to mean there was a change somewhere. There was an 'on and off' switch. Think about all the beliefs you live by. At one point, you had no clue those beliefs existed. How many were being taught science and religions, as a toddler? Most parents were concerned about teaching you how to use the potty, tie your shoelaces, and write your name. Think about it! Those were some of your first beliefs. You did not use the plastic potty, until you believed you could do it. The same with riding a bicycle or swimming in a pool. It was the belief. Something channeled when your family member encouraged you to pedal, while they held the back of the seat. You might have been wearing a helmet or not, but your focus was on your safety. You had enough faith in your family they would keep you from harm, so you were willing to take a chance on the bike. Next thing you know, you were happy with a big smile on your face. And when they saw that smile and confidence, they let go! Picture that. I will need to keep this scenario for later. Although they let go of the seat, you kept riding.

In an instant, something changed. You had enough confidence in your heart that caused a SWITCH in your brain. Next thing you know, you slammed the brakes, looked back, and your family was far away laughing at you. You realized you did not need to be supported and that you could do it on your own. What happened next? You rode back on your own. A change in beliefs happened that fast. You went from doubt that you could ride a bike to a belief you could ride if they held your seat to belief you could do it on your own. See how powerful beliefs can be? This brought me to *Truth*. It was not because I felt I could get rich off the information or I knew more than the next person. It was simply because of my discovery of the power we all possess. I wanted to write this so everyone could be empowered to do more, be creative, and accomplish all our dreams. And when we establish a belief system like this, nothing is impossible.

Let us go back to the beliefs. Remember the bicycle example? There was not a thing or a person that caused you to ride the bike. There were training wheels and family members that encouraged you to ride, but the belief did not manifest itself until there was a change in your thoughts. You created the belief. You created the standard to live by that ultimately altered your life. Before you knew it, you were riding mopeds, motorcycles, and cars. Isn't that amazing within itself? Your small speck of belief in riding a bicycle led you to have the belief you could drive a car. And believe it or not, some people have never learned to ride a bike. There may have been various circumstances that prevented this from happening, while others may have never had the opportunity to be encouraged to do so.

With *Truth*, I want this to change. I never want you to feel you cannot do something you desire to do. I desire to be a living example of what you can do. Stay with me as we dig deeper into discovering who you are and what you possess.

Chapter Three

Who You Are

Humans are amazing beings. If you just look around, you will see how far we have come. No other living being can read these words. Not only can we read and write, but we can do just about anything we can think of. This has been displayed throughout history, time and time again. Somebody thought they could create a device that would allow you to communicate with one another. You could be in another country and I can dial a specific code of numbers that would reach your device. Can you imagine how detailed and precise this had to be? A telephone is nothing more than an imagination. Nothing magical came out of the sky. It was the very idea that led to this huge discovery. I no longer had to handwrite a letter and have it delivered, to talk with you. The creation of pencil and paper was already a huge achievement, but now we had a telephone. This allowed me to talk to you in an instant. At this very moment, I am typing this book on a phone. That is right. The same device that shocked people when they realized they could talk to one another throughout the world is now being used like another major discovery: a typewriter, which advanced to a computer, which can now be held in my hand and go wherever I go. See the transition? See the growth? See the power of the mind?

One of the main reasons we possess this power is how the brain in a human is designed. Compared to other living beings, a human has a denser number of neurons. And although some mammals have much larger brains, we have the largest cerebral cortex, based on brain size. This gives us the ability to generate more conscious thoughts and complex memories. This makes it easy for us to speak languages. This is where you house your thoughts and actions. This goes back to the bicycle. The cerebral cortex helps us remember how to pedal a bike. So, as you go forth with your right foot, you know that you must go forth with your left foot next. This ties to everything we do in life. This type of memory causes us to do certain things without thinking. So much data is stored in the brain that you do not think about which pedal to step on, to move forward. Your memory causes it to be second nature to you. You do not have to remember how to step onto the floor when you get out of bed. You may be so tired that you forget where you are for a moment, but your brain automatically knows to strengthen your feet and legs to lift and sustain the weight of your body. This is the power you hold inside your skull.

The brain's memory plays an important part in our lives, but what initiates the memory? What causes the movement before we learn it? This is what most call the soul, which is you. Think about it. You can look at your foot and move your toes. You are not calling anything to do it. It is simply being done with the soul that the body possesses. The body is only a shell you are housed in. This is one reason it deteriorates, because the body only exists for a specific period. You will notice this as you grow in life. In all honesty, you are the same person you were at 12. You know what makes you think you are not? Your body. The color of your hair has changed, your eyeballs may have weakened, and there is a different amount of energy in your limbs. Therefore, some may say at times that they feel like a kid again. This thought normally changes when you pull a muscle. It is still you. The soul has not changed, just the body. Therefore, we should not focus on outer appearance but focus on you. This alone will help eliminate the doubt and negative thoughts about yourself.

And when we have negative thoughts based on the outer shell, we eventually become it. The negative thoughts and doubts become our beliefs. You are no longer the beautiful soul that could pedal for miles. You are now the outer shell with pain in the right leg and will never get on another bike. It is true. Just as quickly as your beliefs can change on a bicycle, they can change in your everyday life. Do you see that? Do you realize you choose who you are and who you will become? If you want to be a doctor, you can do it. It is an amazing power given to us and most of us fail to use. How often are you letting the outer shell determine who you really are? Despite the health condition or circumstances, it has nothing to do with you! You are a soul. You are not a human being. You are simply housed in a body with a limited amount of time on earth.

And knowing you will only have so much time in this body should be enough motivation to encourage you to do anything you desire. It should cause you to not look back and see if someone is holding your seat but look forward with a smile. Carry the same smile when you were on the bike. That is you. You have not changed. The only change is your thoughts and beliefs. The moment you realize this and place it in your heart and mind is the moment that everything will fall in line. You will no longer think about what you cannot do, but about what you will do. It is a level of confidence that no bicycle can scare out of you. You do not get in your vehicle and say, "I hope I don't get in an accident." At least you should not. If this is your mindset, take a break from behind the wheel and change your focus. Whenever you have this mindset, there is a portion of doubt in your brain and heart. But you just let them stop holding the seat, and now you want to worry?! You mean to tell me you let the outside world change you to where you are afraid to drive? If there is any portion of doubt, even a pinch, you are afraid. So, let us go back.

You are a soul. You are not in your 20s, 30s, 40s, and so forth. You do not change. It must stick to the cerebral cortex. It is impossible to change. The only way you change is through your thoughts, not time. Time cannot touch you. You are still 5, you are still 12. If you make it to 100 years on earth, it is still you! Who cares if your leg does not move fast enough to keep driving? It is still you. Let them drive you around. You deserve it. You remained your true self, so why not get driven around town? Just remember who you are as you move through each decade of your life. Think back. Don't look, just think: "This is me! Ten years later, and this is me. I have not changed. I am wearing glasses, but I like my shell to be looking good. I'm going to make sure I got the best-looking glasses that's available on my face." You did not change, and you will not change.

Do this for me: Stand up and remember who you are. Time on earth and your outer shell have no control over how you feel and think. Remember who you are and who you will always be. I am just a soul communicating with another soul. Do not forget who you are. Serve your purpose and enjoy yourself. The body will eventually leave, but that is the least of your concerns. Never stop being you.

Chapter Four

Communication

One of the most powerful talents we have is communication. Communication is so strong that it alters everything around us, and I mean everything. As soon as you saw the word communication, you thought about the words coming out of your mouth. Talking is important, but it has nothing on how the soul communicates. I learned this on my way to creating this book. It is the key reason I wrote *Truth*. I began to study, research, and learn who we are. And the more I learned, the more I became exposed. Things and situations were showing themselves, more and more. By this time, I had a desire to grow. You should always want to grow and do better. In the process, you can discover your passion and watch it blossom. It got to a point that things happened within minutes. One of the reasons it moved faster is that I got from behind the wheel. In some odd way, the less control I had the more changes I saw. Some situations would frighten people, but my studying and research gave me a different view. I was no longer scared, but I was excited. It was not going exactly like I wanted, but it was going like it should.

Have you ever sat in the passenger seat of your own vehicle and let someone else drive? Even if it was a long road trip, what kind of thoughts did you have going on in your head? I know people that would drive until they were ready to pass out, just so no one else would be behind their wheel. I am telling you now, this is the only way you will reach your desires and goals. Sometimes, you can force the situation, but it usually ends up with a lot of loss and heartache. And sometimes, you can force a scenario never meant to be. All of this happened because you did not want to give up the wheel. Sometimes, you can see where you have messed up. "If only I didn't do it." "If only I had listened." Those were the times you did not get from behind the wheel.

Getting from behind the wheel does not mean doing nothing. You are not sitting on the couch, rubbing a genie bottle. You're not saying, "Genie, take over. I want a big house and a million dollars." Getting from behind the wheel is when you have put in the work and things are not going how you expect it, but you are not forcing it or giving in. An example of not giving in is when I developed a passion to write again and said, "This is what I'm doing." I witnessed my passion stemming from what I was learning. Initially, I wanted to do what I felt comfortable with. One day, a video was on social media about being bold. The lady said, if you are not afraid about what you are about to do, then you are not following your passion. She said there should be some type of concern because you are being bold and going into new territory. That new, unfamiliar territory is what some call "the unknown." Most fear the unknown for that very reason; it is not familiar, and you do not know what may happen. You are not letting anyone drive your car, because you do not know how they will drive what you paid for. There is a huge difference, when you know the person cannot drive.

One of the great teachers I listen to teaches that your blessings will come in ways you least expect. If you have a desire, you cannot force it to be. This is because the way you want it to happen may not be the right way. Your mindset could be based on someone else's achievement or what you have seen on a television show, but things are different in the real world. Nothing is wrong with studying the success of those with a similar vision as you, but do not expect a 'cookie-cutter' life. Once you put in the work and do your part, nothing might happen at first. This does not mean it will not happen, but that it just did not come how you expected. What changes the results is the mindset. When you know it will work and you have done your part, step back and wait. Then, you will witness amazing things happening in your life. People and situations will unexpectedly enter your life to move you closer towards your destination.

And this mindset works in every area of your life, even your health. This is one reason they use a placebo for medical tests. Using a placebo, they will test a new drug on random people. Some will receive the actual drug, while others will receive a tablet with none of the drug in it. Sometimes, people will take the false drug but claim they feel better. This reaction displays that the individual mentally felt better, because they believed they were consuming a pill that would make them feel better. Belief. It was not anything special. It was their belief, their mind. This means you can believe in your heart and mind you will feel better, and it will happen. Your body is a self-sufficient machine that repairs itself. If you have a small cut on your finger, you do not visit a doctor to have the cut stitched and restored. The body knows its job, so it eventually stops the blood and over time heals the finger. You did not have to do anything. All you had to do was believe and let it be. There is a difference if the cut is too large for the body to restore itself. This is when you have the assistance of someone stitching your body together, so it can eventually heal itself.

This is the same with all areas of life. We are souls that communicate with one another. This is how we can instantly feel love, anger, or worry when we encounter someone. These are signals that the other soul can pick up and respond to. Whether the signal is good or bad, determines what the response will be. Imagine if your soul's signal was one of confirmation of your success and growth. When that powerful signal reaches the right people, their soul will easily be attracted and be the very people that make your dreams come true. It all stems back to communication. What are you sending out? Is it a selfish mindset only for yourself? Or is it a powerful vision that can help others be a success as well? The way we communicate is through the soul. Our words are only a result of that communication.

Chapter Five

Meditation

Now that you know how to effectively communicate and manifest your dreams, it is time to prepare yourself for communication. This is done through the teachings of meditation. Meditation is one of the few ways we can clear our minds and be open to what is waiting for us. Therefore, it goes hand in hand with how souls communicate. Before you can ever send out what you desire and communicate it with the right person, you must first make sure there is nothing blocking your line of communication. This blockage could be everything you have been dealing with in the past week: self-doubt, family issues, emotional issues, and so forth. Any of these things can produce negative signals you will unintentionally send out to other souls. This will indefinitely place a hold on your life and any goals you may have. Your next blessing could be right in your face, but you would not know because of the negative signals bringing back negativity.

You can only receive what you send out, so you must focus on positivity. One of the best ways to do this is to have a daily regimen of meditation. The clarification this exercise provides will open your mind to a new world. You will have enlightenment and visions that far exceed what you could ever imagine. You will easily develop a new person. You will correctly inherit the power that was always yours. Meditation has existed for ages. It is one of the only ways some people can find peace, and it continues to be one of the key elements in prayer. What many fail to realize is that your prayers are confirmations that put souls to work. There may be something that you want or need done. But how can you obtain anything in life if your signals never reach the destination? Think about it. Your wave signals are clogged with morning stress, workplace negativity, and personal challenges. So, when you send out your confirmations, all those issues are going along with it. They do not step to the side and wait until you are done. They go wherever you go. Helped by meditation, you are allowing your mind and heart to be clear of anything in your past before you seek what you desire.

Meditation is the key to the door you want to enter. This is one reason people have been healed of issues, through meditation. People have obtained wealth and discovered love. There was nothing in the way of the soul obtaining what they want or need. It is important that meditation becomes a part of your regular schedule. People that regularly meditate do it morning and night, and it only makes sense. You want to start your day with a clear conscious and end your day with a clear conscious. Meditation should be your first and last meal, each day. There are numerous options for meditation. You can start by locating some beginner videos on YouTube, and gradually grow as you learn more. You will see great changes in your life. It will become a habit you enjoy. If you are just starting with meditation, it may take some time before it becomes a daily regimen. Do not worry about that. Everything is a process. The only difference is the length of the process. If you are making it a part of your everyday life, you will get there.

There are some that will not require meditation. I know some great people that rarely use it, but their mind is so aligned with their present because they have no distractions. With the remaining 99% of people, we have more distractions as our lives grow and encounter more experiences. Therefore, meditation is so valuable to our lives.

Chapter Six

Inner Communication

The third part is inner communication. How you communicate in the soul will determine how the story will end. Your words are the final step in communicating. Before you ever say one word, the communication starts within. And if that communication is not right, you are in for a world of trouble. The problem is that most people do it backward. Some believe that what we proclaim will come to be. This is possible, but the inner you has to be aligned.

Therefore, you can shout you will be wealthy and still cry over your last dollar. This results from miscommunication. What you were saying on the outside was not being interpreted on the inside. This goes back to belief. You must believe it will happen, more than you say it will. There is a big possibility that your outer situation is showing something different from what you desire. This is experiencing life in the unknown and not having knowledge in what direction you are headed. Since we are not what is in the outer world, it has no control over what our inner selves choose to do. Unless you allow it to. If you proclaim and believe in something specific and later wonder if it will happen, you have defeated the purpose of having a desire. Words you should never use in your life are maybe, might, hopefully, and possibly. Each one of these carries a string of doubt.

If you even have a drop of doubt in your vision, you will continue to struggle with your vision. I like to use the cup of water scenario. If someone put one drop of rat poison in your water, would you drink it?

If you sat and watch them put one drop in the cup before handing it to you, what would you do? This is the same with your life. Why would you allow one drop of negativity in your dreams or goals? This is where you need to have the inner talk before you move forward. Your inner belief must be so strong that you literally feel it. It is so powerful that you feel yourself in the moment before you ever write the blueprint. You feel yourself healthy, before the doctor visit. This is your inner communication. Not what is on the outside, but what is in the inside. Not what you shout and announce, but what you feel and know. This is where meditation plays an important role as well. When I mentioned meditating and clearing your mind, you are placing yourself in an atmosphere where your mind is open to whatever you desire. You have rinsed it of past negativity and future doubt. You have settled your entire self in the present and planted your future. This leaves no question of what is about to happen. There is not a maybe. There is a will.

The inner communication opens the door. It connects you to the signals you have been seeking. There is someone desiring to provide the finances for a new business. There is someone desiring to sell a beautiful, large home. There is someone desiring to have a clean report for their patient. They just need a connection. You cannot say it, you cannot call it, you cannot only see it. You must feel it. It must be as real as you reading these words. You have no doubt you are reading. You're not thinking: "I may be reading. I might be reading. Hopefully, I am reading. I'm probably reading." You know it for a fact! This is exactly how you must be in your life. Feeling and knowing what you are doing. "I know I'm healthy." "I know my business is successful." "I know I can have that home." This mindset will open doors and change how you look at life.

Many will ask, what is the feeling I speak of? It is like the feeling of excitement when you know something is about to happen. You know your bonus check is about to arrive, so you are already planning how you will spend it. This is the level of confidence you must display. You know in your heart that the check will show up in your bank account. You are not waiting for it to be there. You are planning for it now. Why can't you do this with every desire in your life? This is the main step, separating you from everything you desire to have. One way you tap into this level of confidence is through meditation. The exercise allows us to clear our minds and prepare for our future. It challenges us to fight our doubts and fears. It is an exercise that requires devotion. It is not a quick fix, but it will change your life.

Just remember: What you know and feel may not be what you see. It goes back to what I said about not knowing how your blessing will arrive. It is not meant for you to know. You are not a psychic. You are controlling your heart's desires, not the lives of others. So, it may not always be the person or thing you expect it to be. Do not get discouraged if it is not playing out like a fairytale. Just maintain your vision and get ready for the result.

Chapter Seven

Vision

The vision we have for our lives is an important requirement. How can you communicate if you do not know what to talk about? By the time you reach that point, you should no longer be straddling the fence. This is another issue that can block your communication. You should not be changing goals, every other month. I have made this mistake, so I know wholeheartedly about the indecisive challenges we face. The only problem is that picking up and putting down a goal never allows you time to produce the lifestyle you desire.

Often, we go back and forth because things are not going as planned. The future looks dim, so we put one desire down and chase another. We do not realize this causes us to start over, which will ultimately lead to never accomplishing any goals. You will always experience change in your life, but this is not the change they were talking about. The biggest reason for change is doubt. Do you realize that the main reason people are unsuccessful in life is that they gave up? It was not because the business idea was bad, or they went into the wrong market. It simply concerned believing in yourself. You send out a signal for whatever you believe. As soon as we lean towards doubt, we can expect lack. The channels are simply responding to your beliefs.

Therefore, you must remain true to your passion. If you have an inner desire to do something that will change the world, do not let the physical things deter you. You do not produce in the physical world. This is just the result of what you have already generated inside of you.

You believed it, before you ever saw it physically. Someone knew they could produce the speed of a horse, times 300. Think about that. People were commuting by way of horses, and someone honestly believed they could build a machine that would outrun horses. And this is how we amazingly got vehicles with 'x' amount of horsepower. They never saw a vehicle, prior to this. They simply had the belief they could see it. It started in their mind, it connected with their inner spirit, and has now become the #1 way we commute on earth. Their idea changed the world. And it did not arrive on a silver platter. There was not a special button. They made numerous mistakes, which is a part of life. The difference is their mistakes were not their downfall. Their mistakes became lessons. Now, they knew what not to do. Back to the drawing board, until everything came together. Thomas Edison had the best quote when he said, "I didn't fail. I just found 2,000 ways to not make a lightbulb." Can you imagine having an inner self that strong, where you do not find fault? You just find opportunity. Another person that had a great inner self when they worked was Michael Jackson. MJ said, "I'm really very self-confident, when it comes to my work. I believe in it 100%. I really put my soul into it. I'd die for it." His music was not his outer shell; it was him, his soul. After the success of his Billie Jean album, MJ said he wanted to top it. The next album became one of the highest-selling albums of all-time, Thriller!!

What have you faced in working towards your passion? What mistakes did you make? Did those mistakes cause you to give up? Or did they become lessons that only made you wiser? This is not just for business. This is for life. This same scenario applies to your health, your family, your career. What happened along the way that you felt it was better to give up than learn from the errors? As we know by now, what we send out is what we receive. This means there is not one mistake that can stop you from reaching your destiny. You keep sending out the right channels, you have no choice but to obtain your goal. Sometimes, it can only need one more push from you. Just when you were about to achieve goals in your life, you believed it was impossible and gave up. You no longer knew you could do it. You believed that you might do it. This 'might' was the first drop of doubt. And its power was just like the rat poison that destroyed the water. If you do not address and cancel the negative thought, one drop of negativity eliminates everything that you have worked for. The negative signal connects with more negativity. The additional negativity only confirms the doubt you had, so it multiplies. Before you know it, the poison becomes too strong and kills everything. Five years go by and you forgot about your passion. You settled for what you could see. Now, you spend the majority of your life doing what you can see and not pursuing what you once believed. Now you are just on earth, following a pattern. Doing just enough to live. It does not excite, but it keeps you going. Years have passed and you have more belief in what you never wanted and none in what you once desired.

How is this possible? How do we get to where this is acceptable in life? How do we lose our passion? One way is not having a reminder of why we are here in the first place. Therefore, you need to see your vision. A reminder of what you want for your life. An image and words of encouragement that can override any doubt. This is where it begins. Paint your picture. It could be anything you desire for your life. If it is in your heart, it is your passion. Treat it as so and create a display you can visit and view regularly. Next, surround it with words that define you and the desire you have. Begin the definition with the words, "I Am." Start from the root: "I Am Strong." "I Am Wise." "I Am Creative." "I Am a Creator." "I Am Wealthy." "I Am a Healer." "I Am Abundant." "I Am Amazing." "I Am a God."

Keep building your "I Am," then take those words with you. Keep a note in your pocketbook or wallet, which will remind you every time you see it. You may not even have to open it. Just seeing the folded note will remind you of all the powerful talents you possess. The story of Moses says he believed that he had a higher calling, a deeper passion. Once the passion within him grew so strong, he asked who should he tell the people that the higher calling is. Moses said he was told to say, "I Am." Imagine how much power you are installing, when you proclaim, "I Am." That is why at the very moment I learned the importance of saying I Am, I went for my daily walk and found the words written on the sidewalk. What is more amazing is that I took a route I had never walked before. This is the power of not seeking your blessings and gifts but allowing them to seek you. I received confirmation, without forcing it. It began a journey I could have never imagined.

Start this today: Regardless of your age, situation, or mistakes, you can still pursue your passion, your vision, your ideas, your life. At the same time, feed your brain. Consume knowledge on the things you desire to do. Before you know it, doors will open because you are sending the signals you desire. You are no longer producing the doubt you may have had. Now, you are producing faith and reestablishing beliefs you once had. And when the heart and mind communicate on the same channel, you will see the future before it happens. With a daily regimen of meditation, your mind will remain clear and ready to receive all the new opportunities coming your way. This is how you solidify your vision and obtain everything you want in life.

Chapter Eight

A Leader

Your goal in life should be to lead by example, not lead. Throughout life, we are programmed to believe that we need a leader. There must be someone that holds our hand and guides us in the right direction. Anyone that wants to lead wants control. It is a personal ego, which is the celebrity status of being a leader. A leader comes with its perks. Most people are praised and awarded for being a leader. This may be enticing, but the leader is doing their followers a disservice by leading. We should strive to be teachers. Some of the great people you have heard about in various religious readings were simply teachers. They had no desire to control or lead anyone. They were passing on knowledge to others, while remaining human and not some "better than you" individual. They never chased titles and recognition. It was those that were amazed by their wisdom that placed these individuals on pedestals.

There is a huge difference between leaders and teachers. A leader wears a title and gives orders, while a teacher is an average person simply sharing knowledge. A teacher's goal is to share enough information, so you can become just as wise as them, if not greater. They have no desire to be praised. They do not place themselves on a pedestal. A teacher simply has a passion for teaching. They have a desire to help others grow. We make a mistake when we place these individuals at a higher level than ourselves. Just because they know more about a specific subject than you do not mean they are better than you. Because what they lack in, you may be superior in. This means no one should be leading. Instead, we should be helpers of one another.

By placing someone as your leader, you limit yourself. You have mentally cheated yourself of the talents and capabilities you possess. Someday, you may be better than your teacher. This does not discredit them. This simply means they did an amazing job of passing knowledge onto you. Once this happens, they no longer must be praised. You are the ultimate example of how great they are. Praise is received every time you mention who taught you. Once you remove the title of a leader, you remove limits. You no longer need accreditation from another human being. You have enough belief in yourself to change the world. At the same time, there is no desire to lead others. You should have a passion for teaching the knowledge given to you. This is how 'iron sharpens iron'. You notice it does not say iron sharpening a frail piece of metal. They are equal. The only difference is one possessed strength that the other may not have. But eventually, that iron sharpens the other, until they both are equal. Never look down on yourself or believe that someone is greater than you.

A teacher once mentioned how we are one of the only beings with leaders. They used various animals as examples. When you see a group of fish swimming in the same direction, no one fish is telling the others where to go. All the fish are on the same page, headed in the same direction. Another example is birds. You may have noticed three or more birds flying together. Sometimes one bird may be sticking out further than the others, but it is not the leader. The birds are in agreement and going in the same direction. It is a human that says a leader is needed. If so, then why? Are you saying one is not efficient to be equal with others? Or is that one leader somehow better than everyone else in the group? If this is so, this means that the individual is doing a poor job of utilizing their strengths. Instead of sharpening the others, they would rather keep them at the bottom and never build the success that comes with equality. Imagine how more powerful you are when everyone shares your strengths. How much more can you accomplish when ten of you possess the same wisdom? When knowledge is shared and iron sharpens iron, you are literally multiplying yourself. You now have ten more brains, twenty more hands, twenty more feet, and ten more hearts. You could change the world with this much strength. And it was all done without a leader. Everyone became equal and no longer served each other but helped each other. If you are serving someone or the one being served, you are cheating yourself of the possibilities that surround you. Therefore, we only lead by example. We are not simply leading; it is the knowledge and experiences being taught. We are simply a piece of iron, with a talent of sharpening.

Chapter Nine

Roadblocks

On the way to becoming your true self, there will be some roadblocks along the way. Your roadblocks may differ from others, which is normal. We will go over some of the general roadblocks you may face. You may find some that exist in your life.

Yourself

This will be the toughest roadblock in life. One of the main reasons is that we trust ourselves. Despite what we say or do, we believe in our choices. If we did not have this much faith in ourselves, then why would we be doing this? Good or bad, we always think it is the right decision. This becomes a huge issue when the decision stems from a previous experience. We make a lot of decisions based on our past. But what if the past was horrible, and you want the remainder of your life to be beautiful? You cannot build a future with your past. You must examine self and view where the source of energy is coming from. Are my thoughts, feelings, and beliefs helping me or hindering me? This leads us to the next roadblock.

Past

Past and Present. There is a disconnect between the two. The past may have had negativity. Do you want to utilize negativity to generate positivity? Some use the example of the rose that grew from the concrete. The past makes you stronger. This is true, but that is it!! You lifted weights and gained 10lbs of muscle, but you will not gain another pound from the previous weights. You only gain from now! This means the past should have no input on what happens from now on. The only input is now! What are you doing now? What are you building now? What are you developing now? Now! Most do not want to accept that the past no longer exists, but it is true. Regardless of who was in your life or what you have experienced, it is no longer there. This means you are holding on to false beliefs, an imaginary world. This is a harmful roadblock.

Life

Life comes in a ball, just like the earth. And just like the earth, it has some "not so good areas." The earth in itself is perfect. The same is said for you. You, the soul is perfect. They can only be perfect. How the soul and earth operate is perfection. They must be because they stem from the same source. This makes us one, equally connected. When you have this understanding, the view of your life changes. It no longer becomes a roadblock. When you experience change, it is just that. It is not the end of everything in existence. You still have a goal waiting on you. That minor upset we may view as major has no control over where we are headed. It may slightly change how you get there, but we were not controlling that aspect, to begin with. Right? Truly when you know this deep down inside, you have control over your life. Not the world, not the people, but your life. Who you desire to be, what you desire to have. By not controlling your life, you control your life. What I am saying is the harder we attempt to control everything in our lives, the harder it becomes to control it. There is a level of resistance that strengthens itself, the harder you fight. Because life is doing what you asked for. You want a better life? There is a path you must take to get to that better life. This causes changes to appear to get to what you seek. If you fight the changes, you are ultimately fighting yourself and what you just desired three weeks ago. The resistance kicks in and you are fighting yourself. You are not in control. You are fighting a losing battle. You are fighting and your inner you is fighting back. Who will win if it is you against you? Exactly. Like I said before, it is not the journey but the end result. And when you know the experiences in your journey does not control where you are headed, why would you ever worry for one day? Why would it be a roadblock? When we view life experiences in a negative mindset is when it becomes your roadblock.

Yourself, your past, and your life. It is a lot to clean, but it is not hard. Your thoughts set the arena. It will always be the storyteller. Whatever movie you picture in your head, it will show itself in your life. It is just like dreaming. The only difference is this dream is playing until you leave here, and you have full control, if you desire. As quick as the dream will play out, why not make it the best movie you could imagine? Instead of having roadblocks, have plots where the lead character still wins in the end. With a story this good, you would watch it repeatedly. You would never want to wake up. If this reality is your dream, why waist a moment? Start today. Clear your mind, send out the signal, clarify it, have purpose, and the life you desire.

Chapter Ten

Negativity

Negativity is a seed for destruction. I have witnessed it, time and time again. There are so many people addicted to negativity. We can easily see it in any form of entertainment, from the video games to the television shows to music and even to books. Negativity has the highest rating in entertainment. One reason we love to be entertained by negativity is that we enjoy knowing that others have problems. But this affects us mentally.

You no longer want to watch negative experiences. You start to desire negative experiences. Think about the last time something did not go your way. Do we normally say, "Well, there has to be something good behind all of this"? Most do not. It is easier to say, "If it wasn't for bad luck, I wouldn't have any luck at all." Or the more popular, "It's just a part of life." "It just something we go through." This disturbing mindset will always limit your potential and opportunities. How can you ever prepare for your future if you have allowed your past to harm you? We no longer have access to our past. Not even one second. Think for five seconds. Anything that just happened in those 5 seconds, you can never have back. You cannot say, "Let me go back 5 seconds and change what I did, so things can go my way." The only thing you have is the present. You do not even have the future. The only thing you have is influence on the future. The way you think in the present will alter your path. You cannot control the future you, but you can control the present you. And if the present you has a positive outlook on life, then things not going your way does not stop you from moving forward. You no longer have to pull from a past that no longer exists. Constantly being in the present will clear your mind, restore your health, and generate a positive future.

As mentioned, we send out signals to one another. If your signals are only linked to your past, how could you ever reach what is in your future? You have literally turned your back towards your future to focus on your past. But how? The past is no longer there. If you attempt to look for a previous you, you will never find it. This is one reason our bodies constantly change. We live in a forward-moving life. As a toddler, you were once 1-2 feet tall with no knowledge of what was around you. You can never get that back. That person no longer exists. Life is one long experience. You cannot fast forward it and you cannot replay it. You may watch something that you recorded, but you will never get that experience back. It is no longer real. Now, it is just a video. The video is the only connection with the past. So, why dwell on it?

This is one area that more people need to focus on and learn. You cannot allow the heartache and pain from the past control your present. Whether it happened 5 years ago or 5 seconds, you no longer have it. The normal response is, "This is how I deal with things." With negativity? My response, "This is how you have to stop dealing with things." Would you ever put a hold on your life, income, and well-being for something you can no longer have? It is no longer yours. This is the perfect reason to let go of your past. Yet, most will broadcast their pain and negativity to others. What was once something you can no longer have is now a lifelong platform to spread negativity. In the time you spent dwelling in negativity, you could have been focusing on rebuilding yourself and becoming whole again.

This is the same with our health. Do you realize that a lot of people do not become sick, until they are told they are sick? This is because the cells in our bodies work together. You can think yourself into sickness. From the worry and doubt you feel in your heart and mind, your body responds. It prepares itself for a weaker immune system, being overtaken by cancer, or not having the strength to fight an illness. Afterward, more negativity pours in because your loved ones can sense the negative emotions and they return that negativity with their own worries and doubts about your well-being. Before we know it, we have built a scenario for sickness and destruction. You are no longer channeling success and prosperity. Your life is aligned with negativity and illness, and it is constantly spreading.

The body reacts to you. Like I mentioned in the beginning about the small cut, the body is great at responding. You cut yourself, it instantly responds. You are being chased by a wild animal; it instantly responds. You witness something beautiful and amazing; it instantly responds. If we know the body is this fragile in responding to our mental thoughts, what can we expect from thoughts of being sick or destructive? The body does not see it; you do. The body is simply waiting on your signal. The same way you can be in fear, you can be sick. The body is adjusting to what you delivered. You are preparing for sickness, so it is more fragile to being sick. Therefore, negativity is the deadliest pill on the planet. The good thing is that you have control over it. You have total control. You determine what upsets you or makes you depressed. You determine what worsens your health. If you honestly believe you will be healthy, you will be healthy. Notice, I did not say "can be." You cannot doubtfully believe you can do it. You can only believe and truly feel it within you. Whenever there is a bad experience in life, do not make it a drawn-out, negative timeline. Address the situation, understand it, and change your mind for the better. Always recognize the positive that exists. Sometimes, the positive can just be learning a lesson (what to do/what not to do). Tell yourself that things will be better and believe it in your mind and heart. Tell your loved one that things will be better, and mutually believe it in your mind and heart. And you will witness how miracles happen. There is not a ghost that shows up to your rescue. It is you, the living spirit in a body that aligns itself with the power to change any situation. And when you come into agreement with one another, the change is that much more powerful. All because you chose positive energy over negative. You chose the positive power you possess over the negativity you have experienced. It is that simple.

Chapter Eleven

Limitations

Limitations build walls. I had an experience at a gas station that changed my entire view on life. I discovered how the small things are walls themselves. They may seem petty in the physical realm, but they cause a lot of damage internally. It is the same as a tiny nail on a six-lane expressway. Your massive vehicle is speeding along, and the tip of the tiny nail perfectly aligns with your front wheel. Before you know it, you are at a dead stop on the side of the expressway. It is the same with the small challenges in life. You keep allowing the minor experiences to play a major part in your life, which will place your life on hold as you sit at a standstill along the side.

My gas station experience almost fell victim to this type of challenge. Previously, I set out in my life to be wealthy and grow in my career. By this time, I had written a large amount of this book and I had a better understanding of the true power we have. This meant I had an "I AM Abundant" mentality. This new way of thinking faced a challenge. Internally, it was huge. Externally, it was a petty transaction. It was $2.50. That is right, $2.50 was about to change my entire life!! I stood at the ATM, inside the gas station and was questioning the $2.50 charge for withdrawing $20. In my mind, they foolishly wanted over 10% of what I was withdrawing. It was absurd! I would never let a gas station ATM take that much of my money. My first plan was to search the mobile app for a free ATM, then I discovered something. The lifestyle I desired would not align with the lifestyle I was creating. I could not align myself with people of wealth, being worried about $2.50. Imagine fearing $2.50 but desiring $2 million. It did not add up!

Now, I am not saying foolishly give your money away to receive more money. That is not how it works. You already read about forcing the result. The mind will quickly believe, I will overspend here to get wealth there. No, this is not true. You do not know where this journey will take you, so how can you build a map? It is impossible. Purposely doing things to forcefully manifest your vision differs totally from being in situations where you could alter your vision. I was not searching for the ATM with the highest fee to prove "I AM Abundant." I just wanted $20 to make a quick purchase. The unknown is where all your dreams lie. Everything was unknown, so I was in my area at that very moment. I could quickly get my card back, because $2.50 was too much or I could get what I came for with no concern for the petty fee.

As I got my card back and my $20, I laughed at myself. I witnessed a life that a lot of people experience. I placed a limit on the life I desired. There is no way I could handle a wealthier life with higher expenses. If $2.50 scared me, imagine if my vehicle costs $250,000. I would have passed out, right? It is the exact opposite. We would love to take a ride in that quarter of a million vehicle. If so, this means mentally we must be prepared for it. I told you in the beginning that you must see it before you even proclaim it. You must feel abundance. "A few dollars are nothing for where I am headed." When your mentality is built on lack, then that is your wall. This small transaction had that much pull?? No way. Well, it was not the transaction. It was how the inner me responded if I would have declined. I was no longer pursuing wealth; I was pursuing cheap. So, wherever my signal originally went, this mighty wall within me would have blocked it all. The wealthy prospects for my business might have been eating a $200 meal, which was incompatible with the $2.50 I would have declined.

This is the importance of awareness. Awareness means living in the now, the present. Always be aware of your presence. We will still make some mistakes, but we are still learning. By being aware, I have a greater chance of addressing the former person that would get upset over the ATM fee. I would have called someone to tell them that the gas station is robbing people. The new me, the present me, accepts the charge for this convenience and remain thankful that the ATM was conveniently located. For where I am headed, that is not even a problem, to begin with. But it was a great experience for learning to be the new person I desire to be.

Chapter Twelve

Your Source

One of the teachers I listen to talked about weighing a person, when they die. If you weighed the person just before their death and right after, they would weigh the same. This displays something. This means, you are not the shell you live in. You are a weightless spiritual being that is only housed in the body. This means you can become anyone you desire to be.

Picture that. So many of us limit ourselves to who we think we are. This is one reason I was led to write *Truth*. There are people that have no understanding of who they are. They believe their body is them. And one day, they will leave when the body collapses. Not so. Have you heard stories of people dying, but their heart had not stop beating? Or, they had healthy organs that could be donated to those in need?

This means you are a weightless source of energy, operating this body. Understand there is energy flowing throughout this very existence? Therefore, we can build satellites and grab ahold of the infinite energy and generate phone signals or cable television. Nothing is special about the poles. This energy always exists. We just discovered how to utilize it. So, if the infinite energy is this powerful and you are a part of it, why would you limit yourself? The same way we can grab energy out of the sky and generate images on a television screen, you can grab that same infinite energy and generate your life, your passion, your desire! It is right there. The only issue is only so many know about the power they possess.

The only reason some become hugely successful is they took advantage of their infinite energy. We are functioning off a source. After a period of time, you return to the source you were functioning from. Many religions apply names to the source, but we all live off this platform, this source. This means no one is greater than you. No one is higher than you. You are one with the source, and you can become anyone you desire to be. You want to help less fortunate people, you want to change the flaws in this world, you want to be a writer, you want to be a medical professional, you want to create clothing? You are part of the source, and the source is infinite. The source creates life, and so do you. Limits are what we set for ourselves. Tap into your source:

- The infinite energy is all around us. There is no one being distributing the energy. The energy is everywhere. Therefore, we can pull on that same energy and communicate through phones, devices, computers. It is the same as having energy in your home. You can have multiple objects pulling from the energy in your house. Your microwave is plugged into one outlet of the energy source. Your lights, your washer, your dryer, your television, etc. This is the thing: what the microwave is plugged into does not belong to the microwave. As soon as you unplug the microwave, it is no longer connected, but the energy is still there. You plug a computer into that same energy outlet and now it is receiving the energy that the microwave was once receiving and no longer has! This is us. We are all feeding off this source. It is not ours. It is not coming from a certain area or some being sitting on a throne. The energy is EVERYWHERE! It is infinite!

- This is why animals can live and breathe. Your dog or cat is only living because of this infinite source of energy. The issue is that humans are too smart for their own good, so they attempt to package it and give it a title. No longer is it pure energy throughout this very existence. It is a living being that we can only tap into from a specific place, in a specific way. Every time you inhale, you are receiving that energy. And it is so amazing and unique that you cannot keep what you have just inhaled. The very air you breathe must leave. The energy is everywhere. It is infinite. It is in you! You do not have to call for it. No one calls the satellite signal and ask for it to transmit a TV channel, every time we want to watch something. It is already there. We just learnt how to direct it to televisions. We did not have to pray or bow to the energy, because it is already there. And we clearly know our energy is always present because we are breathing without asking for a thing. How can we ask for something that already exists?? If you do not have to call upon someone for a TV channel, when do you call upon someone for success, peace, health? The source is not man-made. The device to get the source in a specific way is manmade. We did not need a TV to get the energy. We needed the TV to tap into the energy in a different way. You need nothing to get our infinite energy. We just need to tap into it.

- You direct the energy. You reside in the body. You are part of the energy! You are not a person trying to figure out how to use the energy around you. You are the energy!! Think of this. Infinite energy is freely flowing throughout the earth. If it is not put to use, it is useless. We could still not have televisions, radios, cars, homes, microwaves, etc. But we put the infinite energy to use because we reside in shells that include brains to think and create. You are part of the infinite energy. It is not only around you, but it is inside you. So, if you can take free energy in the world and create amazing discoveries, imagine if the same infinite energy is housed inside you. If you are not utilizing this energy, it is useless. You could have built your own plane by now, created your own clothing line or any business, but you vision your world with doubt. You still view yourself as one person. "I'm only one woman." "I'm only one man." You are neither! You are infinite power. If everyone were just one being, how would we ever fly in the sky to visit other parts of the world? It happened because people like me and you utilized their infinite energy. They did not focus on what cannot be done. They placed that magnificent energy on what they wanted done. The rest is history. People have taken trips to other planets! How is that possible if we never had planes to get to the next state over?

- Do you realize there was a time we did not have telephones? We had to write letters. How in the world can you stare at another person living in another country in real-time? We live in different time zones. I can send a text message and you will receive it in an instant! The world did not change! We are the same people that once had only pencils and paper to communicate. The world did not change for us. This energy was available, but our ancestors did not realize it. By coming this far, it means our energy is infinite. It means anything can happen. Not it may or it is possible. It can happen. You have an amazing brain and live off magnificent energy. What is your excuse? Who is forcing you to limit yourself? You have everything in the toolbox, with additional tools on the side. This is the power you possess. This is your source. It needs no name. It is in too many places to have one. This is another reason it has so many packages and names. It is in too many places. It is in every living being. Any living being that has been slaughtered or died of a natural cause, once had the infinite energy. If you are alive and breathing, you are not living off a battery. You can only live and breathe through the infinite energy that encompasses everything. The air we breathe, the plants that grow, the rain that falls are all part of infinite energy. If something this powerful is living inside you at this very moment, you have no excuse. All you have is opportunity. All you have is the magnificent energy of our source.

Chapter Thirteen

Beliefs

Beliefs are the anchors in your life. They determine everything you are and will be. No matter what knowledge, skills, or talents you possess, your beliefs are your result. This means you can have great potential in being a doctor, but if you do not believe it, it will never come to fruition. You can even fight to make it so. You can attend all the classes, watch all the lectures, do all the studying, and still not become a doctor. You never believed you would become a doctor. You were only working towards it because you felt it was the right decision.

Isn't that amazing? Do you see how important a belief is? It goes back to riding a bicycle. You never took the training wheels off because you did not believe you could. The very moment you realized you were riding without the help of training wheels, you believed you could do it in that instant. Some people do not even need to experience riding without training wheels. They just need to see others do it. Their older sibling is doing it with ease. "If they can ride on two wheels, there must be something to this. I know I can ride on two as well." It is the belief factor.

A definition of belief is confidence in the truth or existence of something not immediately susceptible to rigorous proof. This means you cannot prove that it is true, but you believe that it is true. The bicycle scenario shows us this again. No one could prove to you it was safe to ride on two wheels, until you saw it. Initially, it was just a belief. At one time, you did not even know a bicycle existed. It was not until you saw it for yourself that you knew it was real. This goes for every belief in life. Until there is physical evidence, it will always be a belief. "I believe this will happen." There is no way to honestly prove right or wrong, which is why it is a belief. This is also why a belief can be a crutch. If you cannot see it, you can believe that it is there.

Imagine spending your entire life believing something. There is no evidence, so you must choose to either believe or not. This is the gift and curse of beliefs. You can believe something so strong that it becomes you. It is not you. It became you. You no longer believe it. It is you. Think about every belief that exists in your life. At one point in your life, you never knew about it. It did not exist in your world. You could not speak at one point. This means even language did not exist. You had to be taught. This is one reason a cow in English can have a different name in other languages. Realize the power of belief. It is not an animal. In English, it is called an animal. This reality is embedded in those that speak English for so long that it can only be a cow.

What if someone approached you, decades later and said, "We made a mistake? All this time, we were calling this a cow. It was a mooch. We got the two mixed up." This results from a belief. And this has happened in real life. Not the cow scenario, but people being taught to believe something that was only true to them. There was no proof, only a belief. We all know about the "flat earth" phenomenon. People across the globe believed the earth was flat. Could you imagine walking on a 'semi-flat' ground and being told the world was flat? There was no proof it was not, and it was partial proof it was. Who would you believe? Pay attention to the previous question: Who would you believe? This very belief placed people in fear. Do you realize it was people that would only travel so far because they feared their belief? They put their entire lives at a halt, over a belief. They could have experienced life, but the belief became them. It was no longer something they believed in, but it was them. Could you imagine being on your deathbed and learning that the world was round, and you would never go off a cliff? You would be heartbroken! You could have experienced so much more in life. Life would have been so much more fun and not controlled by a belief.

But why? Why would this happen? Belief is neither yay nor nay. It is something to believe in. Until there is proof, it is just something that a person believes. And those that become their belief, no longer need proof. Their belief is all the proof they need because they are their belief. For a long time, people did not believe waves in the air could transport signals. And some believe there were. The difference is someone proved their belief. They did not just simply believe it. So, the first time there was television, some people freaked out! They thought it was the end of this flat earth! They were still trapped in the belief they had become. No one could tell them differently because the belief was them.

Think about every belief in your life. I recommend writing them down. No matter what the belief may be, note it. Some people believe certain things, based on history, age, ethnicity, current situation, etc. Every belief you eventually have seen with your own eyes, write 'yes' next to it. You have physically seen it. I will cheat on this one. If it were not a belief, you would have never written it down. If you had physically seen it, it would not be a belief. Notice, I did not say experienced it. An experience can be a number of things. You can feel a certain way and call it an experience. Hence, phone sex. You can talk on the phone and have an orgasm. Maybe the conversation was so strong that you had an orgasm, but did you have sexual intercourse? You may have experienced sex but did not have sex. Have you experienced what you believe in or is there proof to what you believe in?

Regardless of how old you are and how long you have had your beliefs, do not let a belief stop you from experiencing life. Regardless of your family background or beliefs that existed way before you got here, you can still become who you are. You can still be who you desire to be. If someone tells you differently, it is up to you to believe what they say. Even health situations. Your doctor is just practicing, so it is their belief. It is up to you to believe as well. Whenever someone tells you they believe something, take it for what it is. Acknowledge their belief. You do not have to be disrespectful or call them crazy. If neither of you has proof, you both just have different beliefs. The only problem is when you allow beliefs to hinder this short amount of time you have on this earth.

You can utilize beliefs in the right way! Have beliefs in things that are productive, not things that enclose you in a shell. Not things that separate you. "I believe I can start a business. I believe I can build a machine that flies in the sky. I believe I can become wealthy. I believe I can be healthier." Notice the trend? These beliefs are for good. They are not saying, "I believe I am right, and you are wrong." Nothing is wrong with having a belief but keep it as that. Until the cat jumps out of the ground, it will continue to be a belief. And no matter how good it may sound, do not let it change you. Research, invest some time, learn more. These are all good things. It is only an issue when you make the belief exist in your head, but not in the physical realm. "I will never drink water again, because it is only gas in a clear form." A belief that must be proven is not reality and is not something you should make others believe. Do not discover a belief and make it true. Discover truth and change your beliefs.

Chapter Fourteen

Why Do We Fail

Some of the worst advice someone could give a person is that they must go through pain and failure to succeed. Although it is said time and time again in so many ways, it is the worst lie that could be shared. You may face challenges, but it is up to you to view the challenges as pain. By telling someone that everyone will have a loss to win is purposely preparing them for failure. With this mindset, an individual has trained themselves to believe that they will fail eventually. What type of advice is being shared? Expect failure.

This purposely places failure in your life. The disturbing part is that most people simply pass down what was taught to them. This is how a belief can live so long and eventually become a part of life.

"Everyone has to fall at least once!"

Everyone? What about those that became millionaires by starting a business as a teenager? Those must be the 'lucky ones.' Life would not exist without a challenge. And a challenge exists because it is opposite of what a person wants to do. This makes riding a bicycle a challenge. In the beginning, we wanted the bicycle to balance itself like the tricycle. Once we discovered this was not possible, it became a challenge. We learned why the three-wheel could hold its balance and the two-wheel required our assistance. It was a lesson learned. It was not pain. This is exactly how everything goes in life.

When you discover that the universe adjusts to you, it is impossible for anything to be painful. Think about it. You asked for it! You were a bagger at a local grocery store that desired to be the manager. You have great desires! You want to grow, you want to learn, you want wealth, you want to achieve. Being an individual that manages an entire store differs greatly from an individual that bags the groceries. The management role can be so big that they require an assistant manager. This means the roles are on two levels: vastly different. To become 'management-like', you must have management experience. You have removed the training wheels because you want more control. This means you will have to experience things that a manager has to deal with.

Haven't you heard that a person must see their desires before they manifest it? There is no other way around it. Learning to ride a bicycle has nothing to do with driving a car. They are on two levels. You must see yourself behind the wheel. This is driver's training. If you cannot vision driving 50 miles per hour with cars speeding past you, then you cannot handle being a driver. The same with managing a store. You manage other employees, merchandise, and money. A bagger only learns how to properly fill grocery bags. So, when you plant your desire, the world adjusts to your desire. Everything on earth is obtainable! This means things will enter your life to prepare you for this desire. Experiences and situations you are not used to seeing. It is the only way to change your life and have the life you desire.

Do you realize an experience only becomes a challenge if you fight it? There is not one experience in life that does not happen for your good, unless you purposely chose an experience with negative results. This does not include the normal process of life, such as death. We all know the rules of life. Death is inevitable, and so is change. If we know that we must fight the experience for there to be a challenge, then why would you ever fight against any experience in life you had no control over? Instead of finding a complaint, find the good and realize it is a part of your journey. When you know your goal/destination, every experience in life is a plus. It just moved you that much closer to your destiny. Who could view that as a challenge? Every hour you get closer on a road trip is a gain. "I have one less hour to drive." Imagine how life would be if every experience was a gain. When aligned with who you are and the power you have, you can visually watch as the world adjusts for you. You will witness circumstances you would never have expected. And be thankful you did.

If you did not change, it would mean your life is at a standstill. Either you are content with where you are, or you are fighting too hard because the fighting is placing a pause on life. Realize that the changes had to be made, so fighting against them and viewing them in a negative way would mean you do not want change. If you do not want change, you do not want to be aligned. If you do not want to be aligned, then you never wanted your desires. Now that we know desires require alignment and alignment means change, where is the pain? We have simply labeled the changes in life as pain or problems. Every unexpected change that enters your life are little nuggets of gold! You may want to triple your income. Do you realize how closer you just got, after the last experience? Do you realize that you cannot fail when you desire to succeed? The next time something unexpected happens in your life, proclaim, "I had the most amazing experience, today!" It could be going 30 minutes outside of your route home from work due to construction and witnessing a vacant building for sale. If every unexpected change is viewed as negative, then you just lost 30 minutes of your day. If everyone is a gold nugget, you just found a potential location for your business. This is the power you have. When you respond to life with the mind to always win in any situation, you can only win.

Chapter Fifteen

Brain Power

How do you view the brain? In general, we place a lot of value in the brain. For some, we invest more in the brain than our actual being. Before you know it, you have all this power absorb in this tool, which will alter how you view life. This is one way the brain can either help you or destroy you. The main reason the brain can cause harm is by what it absorbs.

Our brains have been absorbing information, since the first day. This is how we learn how to eat as an infant, communicate, and interact with others. Our memories create our view of the present, but a brain absorbs just like a sponge. When you clean with a sponge, it does not choose what it will and will not take in. When you clean a dish, the sponge does not only take in the soapy water and leave out the dirt or grease. Visualize the last time you cleaned a skillet. When you turned the sponge around, the typically bright yellow was now a brownish, dark color. It absorbed everything!

The brain does the exact same thing. It absorbs your positive and negative experiences. Regardless of how good or bad it may have been, it holds a residence in your memory. If this is true, how will you approach new experiences? If you visited a chain restaurant and found hair in your food, how will you view that restaurant at a different location? Better yet, what will you tell others about the restaurant? The negative experience is housed in your brain. Therefore, the brain can hurt you or help you. This does not mean you should forget about the hair. The hair is just one example, but what about the negativity that travels throughout the brain daily?

It has been estimated that a person has 60,000 or more thoughts in one day and for most people, at least 90% is rehashing past experiences. Can you imagine that? Can you picture yourself thinking past experiences 54,000 times? When would you have the opportunity to think about the present moment? This is one reason one bad relationship can cause a person to never trust another relationship in their life. There is too much negativity about the past affecting your present. People will say, I do not think negative 54,000 times a day. Most of your thoughts happen unknowingly. They bypass without your recognition or approval. The brain has so much to go off that it never stops. It just freely flows. We have allowed it to happen for so long that we have accepted it as a part of life.

This is the true power of the brain. There is no issue with having wisdom and knowledge. The issue is not having control. If you cannot sit for 60 seconds without having a thought, then the brain controls the domain; not you. It is understandable because we are rarely taught about managing the brain. We are trained to focus on filling the brain, and the brain is a never-ending sponge. It will take everything you give it, which is why it remains to be the most powerful source of information on the planet. People are still attempting to mimic the power of the brain, with no success. If a brain is that strong, it would only make sense to control it and not just feed it. If feeding the brain is powerful, think of how stronger you could be when you control that power.

By now, we should understand that we are beings in a body. This means that everything this body can do is useless if you did not reside in it. The eyes cannot read this information without you. When the living being departs, the body collapses. It does not matter how many accolades you had, prior to the departure. Knowing you have this much power, there is no reason the brain should be running the show. You should be addressing every negative thought that attempts to pass by, because you will eventually have a negative view on life in general. Life is one long gift. Nothing is bad about life. There may be bad experiences, but when they happen, they leave. Your past does not exist. At this very moment, you are reading. Anything you may have experienced in the past is no longer real. You may have the thoughts of what you have experienced, but that is it! That thing, person, or incident is not real. You cannot touch the situations that happened in your life. They happened. They are not happening. Your situation could result from what happened, but that is up to you. You keep linking the present to the past. Every single second is new. As soon as you say now, it leaves. You have to say now, because the previous now no longer exists. This is how real life is. It restarts every second. You only live in the present. The future and past are not real. They are only your imagination. Your thoughts and the brain are delivering 60,000 or more experiences, every day.

Now, it is time to control those thoughts that channel the brain. No longer allow the brain to determine how life is or how it will be. There is no way to determine what will happen in the future, so playing out scenarios in your mind is obsolete. Instead, you can address any negativity. Do not forcefully try to stop the negative thoughts, because everything on earth reacts like a magnet. The power increases, the more you try to fight it. Instead, focus on clearing your mind and limiting the negative thoughts. One of the best ways to limit negativity and eliminate it is through meditation. Meditation clears the mind, which allows you to have an open canvas to paint any picture you want in your life. This means you can have a mindset of only happiness and success. Who would not want to live in bliss 24/7? Who would not want complete control and not be victim to negativity? You achieve this when you control the brain and its power.

Chapter Sixteen

Affirming

An affirmation is when you affirm something in your life and/or situation. It partially takes you out of the physical realm because we realize we cannot base our desires on what we see. It must be planted on what we know. The beauty of an affirmation is that it can be a reminder as you remain on your journey. You can have 60,000 or more thoughts pass through in a day. Wouldn't that make it difficult to keep focused on your desire? I have seen this in my own writings. I will have an idea for a new book, put a little down on paper, then forget about it. It was not because I was not willing to give my all or I thought about it half-heartedly. I simply had 59,999 other thoughts that required my attention in 24 hours. This book proves it. I was writing two books at one time. I had an idea for one book and as I was writing it, an idea for another book came along. The mind is so enhanced that it can form a new project, while working on a project.

So, we write down our affirmations; especially if you have more than one. Or, if you have a social media account. Trust me, distractions far outweigh focus. I place affirmations on my desk, on my phone's wallpaper, take screenshots, and even record myself verbally stating the affirmations. Recording yourself is unique, because you can hear the affirmation, and you hear yourself speak them. What could be more powerful? You are replaying yourself proclaiming your destiny. Some people even play their affirmations, while they are asleep. When you are in a deep sleep, you are completely closed off from the world around you. This limits the distractions and allows whatever being planted to firmly take hold. On top of that, you hear yourself confirm it. This is another way to build confidence in your destiny. Before you know it, it could become a norm for you. The affirmations found a home amongst the many thoughts, while cutting out distractions and doubt.

Your affirmation can be anything you desire in your life. There is no right or wrong way to affirm your vision. Some simply write a list (e.g., better job, bigger home, relationship). Some may personify their affirmation (e.g., I want a bigger home, I will get the management position, I Am Abundant). I would recommend not being too general with an affirmation. You could affirm a better job, but what is a better job for you? Is it a specific occupation, higher position, or with a certain organization? You want to focus on the desire, so you do not come up short. I recently learned how others add uniqueness to their affirmation by putting them in a rhyme (e.g., "I have a wonderful business that promotes better health, beneficial products that generate wealth"). I liked the creativity behind this idea because the rhyme can make it easier to remember. Once I discovered this, I placed a rhyme to my own affirmations: "I have awesome books that entertain feelings, euphoria literature that generates billions." There is no right way. If it maintains the desire within you, the affirmation is benefiting your life.

At the beginning of this chapter, I stated how affirmations partially take us out of the physical realm by placing our focus on the desires and not the world around us. It is partial because you must do the remaining part. An affirmation can be anything you want it to be. You can say, "I Am a Bird!" Nothing is wrong with proclaiming it if you believe it. Proclaiming words with no substance is a total loss. If you do not know deep down this will happen, the words will do nothing for you. Ultimately, an affirmation is just confirmation that can be a daily reminder. It generates nothing. It will always be you that creates the reality, not an object or thing. Rereading that "I will have a better job" and dread walking into my current job is a positive and a negative. They cancel each other out. This affirmation was confirming a joyful employment, while my mindset was wrapped up in a negative employment. See the issue? You cannot eat your food, and then prepare the meal. The meal must be prepared first. This is the function of life. Nothing goes backward or out of order. So, you cannot get the job and then be a joyful worker. The joy must be there, for the employment to ever find you. It is not searching for beings that are in hate. When you become what you want to be, you will never have to search for it. Be the affirmation you desire, and you will be pleasantly reminded for the rest of your life.

Chapter Seventeen

Instant Change

This covers everything that pertains to life. This book was written, courtesy of a being. A living being. In the books, we are labeled as human beings. We are beings within a human. The human is the home on earth, the shell. It houses the being, me and you. When a human body develops, it starts like a tiny beetle. You would never know it was a human in its beginning stages. Over time, the organs develop, and the body takes form. With all the magical chemistry and art that takes place in a woman's womb, this creation only obtains its importance from the living being that resides within it.

A child in the womb could have a perfect heart, lungs, brain, and kidney that have never been exposed to harm, and yet have no place on this earth without a living being inside them. From the first day, you are this important. You are the being. And to make it even more magical than the creation of a child; you were always here. You were always being. You just needed a human to be created, so you would have your home. The man and woman do not create you; they create the body. There are not millions of beings floating in our bodies, waiting to be called upon. There is only one source. And we have been given the ability to procreate human bodies for this source. We are living beings. No being can procreate unless they are alive. Anything dead has missed their chance. This is how important it is to have this opportunity to reside in the now, at this present moment.

And just like you do not have millions of beings housed inside you, you are not one out of the trillions that had an opportunity to experience life on this planet. It is only one that exists. When you produce a living child, you are simply extending who you are. You did not start something new. It was already there. If you had no child, someone else would have one; and there is life. There is the source. The only difference we have, between each other, are the bodies we reside in. Because I look so different from you, you separated and viewed yourself as one and only. You truly are one of a kind, because the body is temporary. The world will never see you again when it is all said and done. But this is externally. This is a temporary frame. When we channel into the inner being, you discover that you exist forever. This does not mean you will die and come back to replay it all over again. This would falsify that you can no longer have your past back. You will return, but you will not have your parents, cousins, best friends, co-workers, and so forth. You will return as who you are originally, a part of the source. If every living child could understand this in the beginning, there would be a better understanding about life. You are a portion of this very existence. Every single life that has lived on this planet is you. You just existed in another form. This includes animals. They are a part of the source and should be treated as such. Every living being entered this world, like me and you. Therefore, we all are important.

This is how important it is that you live for right now because this experience only happens once. It is necessary to understand how special this moment is. When we know the miraculous moment in existence, how could we ever become concerned with the past? How could we ever stress about what may happen in the future? We would miss what is taking place at this very priceless moment! Right now. See where you are. Realize the gift to be in this present moment. This is why we are called beings. We are simply being. There is no time. We base time on how the physical operates. The body only exists for a period of time, then it deteriorates to the soil like every other physical form. The source is not affected by it. This eliminates 'the end of the world' scenario. It is impossible. Maybe life as humans could end on earth someday, but it would just return as something else. This is one reason we should not stress over what comes. The worries about "what may be" strip us away from the gift we have now. How will you value this opportunity? This way, future worries would never come to be. If we value the gift we have now, when would there ever be pain, hurt, or destruction? It is impossible! You are too focused on the magnificent now. This means now can never go sour. The second you take your concern off now is when you allow it to fall and be a painful experience. This is how important a being is. You determine now.

If you are happy now, guess what happens in the next now? It will always be now. If you can grasp this, everything you desire in life is in front of you. You are not questioning it. You are living in it. This is the whole point behind manifestation. You simply do not have, because you are not controlling your current experience. If you want to be abundant in the future now, what do you have to do in the current now? You want wealth? You want love? You want to travel? It is happening now. As you read this, someone is taking a jet to a private island. It may be you. The only reason they are experiencing this is that they changed their now. It is the only thing we have. Anything that is labeled the future is simply a future now. It is now. You can never move one second ahead of time and call it the future. As soon as you attempt to say future, it is now. Therefore, time is not your concern. Time is not real. We use time for the things we have created in the physical realm, but it will never control who you truly are unless you allow it. The moment you base your now on time, circumstances, past, or potential future, you lose it all. You no longer have the present. You have what you imagine it will be. This is living in a false reality. Do not imagine what life may be or should be. Imagine how incredible life is. Live in the moment. Take advantage of the opportunity of being and simply be. This key will give you access to any door you desire to open.

Gratitude

We are allowed this short moment in these shells to be whatever we desire. That, within itself is a gift. It is the greatest present we could ever ask for. This is one reason to totally live in gratitude. Imagine having a mind always thankful. Thankful you can wake up. Thankful you can read these words. Thankful you can still see one another. Thankful you can still be whatever you desire. Thankful you can still have whatever you desire. If every being lived in gratitude, where would the flaw be? And the amazing part is that this is possible, because there is at least one thing to always be thankful for.

When you are grateful, there is no lack. There are no issues because you are no longer focused on negativity. And when your mind is only focused on positivity, more positivity will follow you. Before you know it, you will only be grateful because more goodness will enter your life. This is true abundance. And you can never force it. You cannot find it. You cannot ask for it. You cannot build it.

You can open a grocery store. You can start a clothing company. You can become a CEO. You can even purchase your own island. But you can never obtain abundance. Abundance comes to you. Abundance searches for you. Abundance is everywhere. It just needs the opportunity to enter your life. It just needs a pure heart. Abundance is not money, cars, houses, family. It is growth. Living abundantly is living a growing life. So, all these things can result from abundance. Therefore, you do not chase after these things; you seek growth. Growth and abundance are the same. You grow in gratitude, you become abundant.

Do not take this the wrong way. Like I said about the ATM scenario. You are not purposely spending more to obtain more. You are not purposely being thankful to become abundant. You cannot "play the role" with abundance. Our source is not a physical being that is watching your every move and responding to kind gestures. The source of our very life is you! It is you. This means you must be pure. "I want to be gratitude." Just be. Be thankful for life. Do not be thankful to obtain more. Truly be. When you put on a show, you are only lying to yourself. Do you understand who you are?

You are the source. You cannot play the role in one setting, then be someone else in another. You only fooled yourself and remained in the same situation. You only live in the now. So, if you want to change your now, you must change who you are being. Therefore, becoming gratitude is so important. Once you realize who you are, you should only want to be gratitude. You start to truly experience life. Being one with source and being grateful for this opportunity becomes noticeable to the abundance. You are growing in your awareness. And growth is what?

They are the same! If you have not grown throughout life, then you will never experience abundance. Every day you should be growing. It need not be huge leaps, unless that is where your heart and desire lie. Always remember, there are no limits. Simply be. This is what we are. We are beings. You can start today. Start being gratitude. Learn to appreciate life and the existence that surrounds you.

Chapter Eighteen

Who You Are

I have listened and studied so many great teachers during this amazing journey. One of the key teachers is a gentleman named Wayne Dyer. Dr. Dyer has so many great writings and lectures, and I highly recommend obtaining some of his work. I discovered Dr. Dyer through the world of YouTube. It was interesting to learn that Wayne Dyer was raised in the same state as me. He died at a young age, so I never met him. The knowledge he shared still affected my life. It makes total sense when he spoke about not letting your song die with you. He constantly spoke about this in his work. Because Dr. Dyer died at a young age, we would have missed out on the knowledge he had to share if he had allowed his song to die with him.

This very commitment is motivation for myself, and I hope it is motivation for you. There is no way I could allow this song to die with me. Dr. Dyer said we all have a song within us. Every person on this earth. It is all about finding your passion and pursuing it. Sharing it with the world, before it is too late. You never want your song to die with you. Just like Dr. Dyer, your song can far outlive you. It can change someone's life. Imagine what he could be thinking at this moment if he were alive. Seeing how a man in another generation is being influenced by words shared decades ago. It fits perfectly.

Dr. Wayne also gave me the inspiration for "I Am." I still remember listening to his teaching as I worked. He taught about how powerful those two words are. By simply saying "I Am," you are applying something to your life. I got lost in the information. In the afternoon, I went for my walk on my lunch break. As I said earlier in the book, I took a different route than I would normally take. I just felt different. I was still listening to the lectures as I walked. I remember making a left, down a sidewalk. I happen to see colorful words written in chalk on concrete. Unknowingly, I was walking in the opposite direction. I saw words that said, Strong, Smart, Kind, Happy, and so forth. When I got to the end of the trail of words, my eyes widened in amazement. The last two words written on the sidewalk said I Am. It applied to all those powerful words I had just read. It was confirmation of my new understanding. "I Am Strong. I Am Smart. I Am Kind. I Am." We have all these opportunities lying before us, and all we must do is say "I Am." Imagine the wealth, the greatness, the peace, the harmony. When added to your life, you become these things. You become your destiny. You become your greatest desire. It is here. It is you. All you ever must do is say with belief, "I Am."

I Am Love

The best way to end this book is on love. This is the rock for everything! If you have ever needed peace in your life, this is it. Just add it by saying, "I Am Love." Find something to write with and write on, then write your affirmation. You can also place this on your mobile device. Once you place that seal on what you know to be true, you have everything else. You already realize that we live in the now. So, whatever you plant in the now, you will have in the now. Two weeks from this moment, you will be in the now. It is that easy and that pure. As I previously mentioned, we are perfection. The flaws that exist do not control the real you, which is the inner self. Nothing can harm it. So, if you want to plant love, expect love from here on out. It moves that perfect. Hate only exists in a lack of knowledge. Knowing who you are allows you to have it now. There is no category. You have access to everything. And those that are in love have access in abundance. Some of the greatest givers are the wealthiest. This is not just financial wealth or financial giving. You connect with what you send out. You want peace in your home, state your "I Am." At the same time, know who you are. Realize that you are changing your now at this very moment! You are changing the rest of your life.

Now, you may perform the "I Am Love" meditation. The best way to enter this amazing experience is with meditation. A fresh, clean mind that can absorb this affirmation into your everyday lifestyle. I previously recommended meditating twice a day. This is a meditation you can make a part of your regular schedule. Please set aside time for the "I Am Love" meditation.

Acknowledgements

A special thank you to the numerous family and friends that support my dream and building this writing career. Thank you to those that have been there since day one and thank you to the those that discovered my passion and has supported me ever since. It is because of people like you that I continue to write and grow.

A special thanks to my book coach, Precious Brown, and the entire Book to Business family for making this project a huge success.

A special thanks to my book designer, Snirz94 on Fiverr. Thank you for the quick, polished work, and the friendship that has developed.

Always, thanks to my parents for the man that I have become and your undying support.

And most importantly, thank you to my wife and family for being the reason that I strive to provide only my best in every project that I do.

About the Author

Nicholas had a talent for writing when he penned his first fiction book, which was the first book in the White Collar Woman series. He knew the original book was only a layer of where he could go with his writing. Never knowing that his true gift was still waiting inside. Along with the amazing support that surrounds him, he went on to write several books before TRUTH. Outside of his books, Nicholas lends his writing craft to other forms of inspirational content. This includes blogs on his websites and other nonfiction literature.

He was born and raised in Michigan, while enjoying traveling and experiencing the many gifts this world has to offer.

More Information About Future Releases:

VISIT

WWW.WHITECOLLARWOMAN.COM

EMAIL

nicholas@whitecollarwoman.com

Made in the USA
Coppell, TX
29 October 2020

40462025R00060